MILITARY VEHICLES

BY **JANET SLINGERLAND**

NORWOOD HOUSE PRESS

Cover: Vehicles carry groups of soldiers on missions around the world.

Norwood House Press
P.O. Box 316598
Chicago, Illinois 60631

For information regarding Norwood House Press, please visit our website at: www.norwoodhousepress.com or call 866-565-2900.

LIBRARY OF CONGRESS CATALOGING-IN-PUBLICATION DATA

Names: Slingerland, Janet, author.
Title: Military vehicles / by Janet Slingerland.
Description: Chicago, Illinois : Norwood House Press, [2018] | Series: Vehicles on the job | Includes bibliographical references and index.
Identifiers: LCCN 2018003247 (print) | LCCN 2018007259 (ebook) | ISBN 9781684042272 (ebook) | ISBN 9781599539430 (hardcover : alk. paper)
Subjects: LCSH: Vehicles, Military--Juvenile literature. | Armored vehicles, Military--Juvenile literature.
Classification: LCC UG615 (ebook) | LCC UG615 .S57 2018 (print) | DDC 623.74--dc23
LC record available at https://lccn.loc.gov/2018003247

312N—072018
Manufactured in the United States of America in North Mankato, Minnesota.

CONTENTS

Note: Words that are **bolded** in the text are defined in the glossary.

The military relies on vehicles that move soldiers from water to land.

CHAPTER 1

FROM SEA TO SHORE

A large metal vehicle sits on a ship.
It heads down a ramp. It glides into the
water. Waves make it bob up and down.
Then it heads for shore.

The vehicle drives up the beach.
It climbs over a sand dune. It picks up
speed on level ground.

It stops at a safe spot. A ramp at the back lowers. Soldiers run down the ramp. They are ready for action!

The vehicle is an **amphibious** assault vehicle, or AAV. The AAV looks like a tank. It runs on **tracks**. It has mounted guns. It drives on land. But unlike a tank, it also floats in water.

A crew of three **marines** handles this AAV and its guns. Up to 25 more soldiers ride in its belly. They use the AAV to move from sea to shore.

The Marine Corps uses AAVs on missions around the world.

Soldiers go in and out of this IFV from its rear doors.

CHAPTER 2

PEOPLE MOVERS

Soldiers make up an army. It takes many vehicles to move soldiers from place to place.

The army relies on various types of Infantry Fighting Vehicles (IFVs). An IFV moves squads of soldiers into battle.

STEM AT WORK: CAMOUFLAGE

Many new military vehicles look like they drove out of a video game. They have **pixelated camouflage**. Instead of curvy blotches of color, they have lots of little blocks of color. These blocks help mimic textures found in nature. So, it takes our brains longer to spot them.

A squad usually has four to ten soldiers. An IFV has armor. This protects soldiers from enemy fire.

On the battlefield, an IFV's weapons also protect the soldiers. Most have machine guns. Some have cannons.

Most IFVs have tracks. They can move well over soft ground. Some IFVs are even amphibious. A few IFVs have wheels. These vehicles can go farther than tracked IFVs before needing more fuel.

Wheeled vehicles are also faster on roads than tracked vehicles.

The Armored Personnel Carrier (APC) also moves soldiers. Its armor helps protect them. It has few weapons. It brings soldiers to the battle. It is nicknamed the battle taxi.

APCs get places in many different ways. Most have wheels. On roads, they can drive as fast as a car on the highway. Many APCs are amphibious.

APCs can carry soldiers through dense forests and across rough ground.

The US National Guard uses LMTVs to take supplies to disaster areas.

CARGO VEHICLES

The military moves more than just people. It ships food, water, and medicine. It hauls weapons and **ammunition**. It moves big things like shelters and bridges. There are many vehicles that do these jobs.

The four-wheeled Light Medium Tactical Vehicle (LMTV) is a **cargo** truck. It brings supplies to camps. It moves equipment as well as soldiers.

An LMTV can carry over 2 tons (1.8 metric tons) at a time. That's about the weight of a car. A crane can attach to the truck. This loads and unloads heavy things.

A Heavy Equipment Transporter System (HETS) can move even larger loads. It can carry tanks! The HETS can haul up to 70 tons. That's as much weight as ten large elephants! Hills and rough ground won't stop this tough truck.

Sometimes soldiers need a bridge to cross water or another obstacle. A special vehicle called a Wolverine can carry a bridge on its back! Within five minutes, the bridge is in place for tanks and other vehicles to use. Once these vehicles have crossed, the Wolverine gathers up the bridge in under ten minutes.

The Wolverine's bridge is so strong it can support a tank.

Soldiers practice driving the M1A1 Abrams tank on different terrain.

CHAPTER 4

FIGHTING MACHINES

A battle tank is an important weapon for an army. It is heavily armored. It rolls along on tracks, allowing it to cross different **terrain**.

A tank has one large gun that can spin around in a full circle. A tank can have several machine guns, too.

ON THE JOB: VEHICLE MECHANICS

The military needs lots of mechanics. Mechanics are problem solvers. They have to figure out what is wrong with a vehicle. And they have to know how to fix it.

Each mechanic works on certain types of vehicles. Some work on tracked vehicles. Others work on wheeled vehicles. Some focus on one specific vehicle, such as the Abrams tank.

A crew of soldiers operates a tank. Maps and plans tell them where to go. The crew moves the tank into position and finds their target. Then, they aim, load, and shoot the gun.

The Multiple Launch Rocket System (MLRS) packs lots of power. This truck can shoot up to 12 rockets in about a minute. Then it drives away quickly.

Before the rockets hit their faraway target, the truck is gone. They call this "shoot and scoot."

The MLRS carries a variety of missiles. Some destroy buildings or **bunkers**. The MLRS can also shoot two long-range guided missiles. These missiles can hit a target up to 186 miles (300 km) away.

The MLRS has a computer that helps it aim at a target.

CHAPTER 5

UNMANNED VEHICLES

Some of the newest military vehicles need no driver's seat. These are unmanned vehicles. They are designed to help save soldiers' lives.

Most of these vehicles are remotely operated. Operators control them from a safe place. Small robots go in to scout an area. Other robots search for bombs. They can then **disarm** them. Operators use video game controllers to move the robots' arms.

Some vehicles can move completely on their own. The Squad Mission Support System, or SMSS, can do this. This six-wheeled vehicle looks like

An SMSS can travel over rough ground.

a heavy-duty cart. Soldiers use it to carry their equipment and supplies. This includes their heavy packs, food, water, and weapons.

The SMSS uses a sensor system to see where it is going. It can follow a soldier or vehicle. It can also be programmed to travel to a specific place.

These and other vehicles help soldiers and keep them safe. The military relies on them to get its jobs done every day.

GLOSSARY

ammunition (am-yuh-NIH-shun): Things that are fired from weapons.

amphibious (am-FIB-ee-us): Able to be used on land and in water.

bunkers (BUN-kuhrz): Buildings that are built mostly underground to keep soldiers safe from attack.

camouflage (CAM-oh-flahzh): A disguise, such as a painted pattern, that helps an object blend in with its surroundings.

cargo (CAR-go): Items moved from place to place on a ship, plane, or truck.

disarm (dis-ARM): Take away a bomb's fuse, making it safe.

marines (muh-REENZ): Members of a military group trained to operate on land, at sea, and in the air.

pixelated (PICK-suh-lay-ted): An image shown as blocks like in a digital image.

terrain (teh-RAYN): A certain type of land, such as rocky ground.

tracks (TRAX): Two continuous belts on which a vehicle, such as a tank, moves.

FOR MORE INFORMATION

BOOKS

Hansen, Grace. *Military Amphibious Vehicles*. Minneapolis, MN: Abdo Kids, 2017. This book looks at the different kinds of military vehicles that move through water and on land.

Riggs, Kate. *Armored Vehicles*. Mankato, MN: Creative Education, 2016. This book introduces readers to armored vehicles and their features, crews, and roles in battle.

Tank: The Definitive Visual History of Armored Vehicles. New York: DK, 2017. This book gives a visual history of the tank from World War I to today.

WEBSITES

American Military Museum
www.tankland.com/vehicles
This page has photos of some of the tanks held at the American Military Museum in California.

Tank and Ordnance War Memorial Museum
www.aaftankmuseum.com/exhibits
This page shows some of the tanks and other military vehicles held at the Tank and Ordnance War Memorial Museum in Virginia.

INDEX

ABOUT THE AUTHOR

Before writing books, Janet Slingerland was an engineer, working on the computers that make things like telephones and airplanes work. She lives in New Jersey with her husband, three children, and a dog.